Global Cities

NEW YORK

Sally Garrington
photographs by Chris Fairclough

CHELSEA HOUSE
PUBLISHERS
An imprint of Infobase Publishing

New York

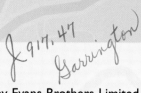

Copyright 2006 © by Evans Brothers Limited

Chelsea House
An imprint of Infobase Publishing
132 West 31st Street
New York NY 10001

Library of Congress Cataloging-in-Publication Data
Garrington, Sally.
  New York / Sally Garrington ; photographs by Chris Fairclough.
    p. cm. -- (Global cities)
  Includes bibliographical references and index.
  ISBN 0-7910-8853-7 (acid-free paper)
  1. New York (N.Y.)--Juvenile literature. I. Title. II. Series.
  F128.33.G37 2006
  974.7'1--dc22

2006045486

Printed in China

10 9 8 7 6 5 4 3 2 1

This book is printed on acid-free paper.

Designer: Robert Walster, Big Blu Design
Maps and graphics: Martin Darlinson

All photographs are by Chris Fairclough except the following, courtesy of Corbis: 12 top, 45 top right, 50, 51, 55 top.

First published by Evans Brothers Limited
2A Portman Mansions, Chiltern Street, London W1U 6NR, United Kingdom

Contents

Living in an urban world

As of 2007 the world's population will, for the first time in history, be more urban than rural. An estimated 3.3 billion people will find themselves living in towns and cities like New York, and for many, the experience of urban living will be relatively new. For example, in China, the world's most populous country, the number of people living in urban areas increased from 196 million in 1980 to more than 536 million in 2005.

The urban challenge...

This staggering rate of urbanization (the process by which a country's population becomes concentrated into towns and cities), is being repeated around much of the world and presents the world with a complex set of challenges for the 21st century. Many of these challenges are local, like the provision of clean water for expanding urban populations, but others

are global in scale. In 2003 an outbreak of the highly contagious disease SARS demonstrated this as it spread rapidly among the populations of well-connected cities around the globe. The pollution generated by urban areas is also a global concern, particularly as urban residents tend to generate more than their rural counterparts.

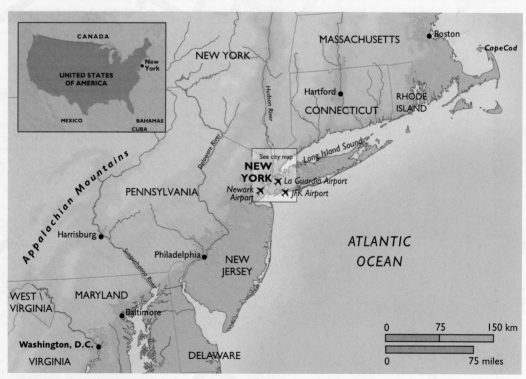

▲ New York in relation to the cities and states of the northeastern United States.

... and opportunity!

Urban centers, and particularly major cities like New York, also provide great opportunities for improving life at both a local and global scale. Cities concentrate people and allow for efficient forms of mass transportation like subway or light rail networks. Services too, such as waste collection, recycling, education, and health care can all function more efficiently in a city. Cities are centers of learning and often the birthplace of new ideas, from innovations in science and technology to new ways of day-to-day living. Cities also provide a platform for the celebration of arts and culture, and as their populations become more multicultural, such celebrations are increasingly global in their reach.

▼ Manhattan, the heart of New York, is a world center of business, finance, and culture.

The boroughs

New York is made up of five boroughs: Manhattan, Brooklyn, Queens, the Bronx, and Staten Island. The most famous of these is the island borough of Manhattan, where most of the famous tourist sites are located. The Bronx is found to the north of Manhattan across the Harlem River, on the mainland. Queens and Brooklyn are at the western end of Long Island—Queens to the north and Brooklyn to the south. Finally, Staten Island is located south of Manhattan Island opposite south Brooklyn. Beyond these boroughs is the New York metropolitan area, which includes part of the states of New York, New Jersey, and Connecticut.

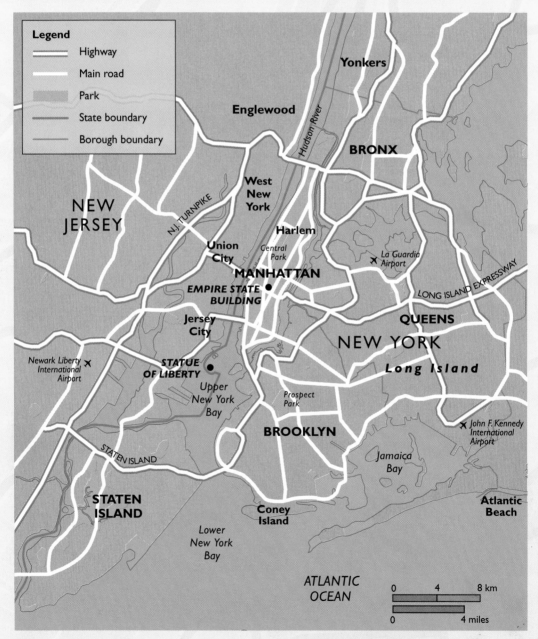

Legend
- Highway
- Main road
- Park
- State boundary
- Borough boundary

Yonkers

Englewood

Hudson River

BRONX

NEW JERSEY

West New York

N.J. TURNPIKE

Harlem

Union City

Central Park

La Guardia Airport

MANHATTAN

EMPIRE STATE BUILDING

LONG ISLAND EXPRESSWAY

Jersey City

QUEENS

NEW YORK

Newark Liberty International Airport

STATUE OF LIBERTY

Long Island

Upper New York Bay

Prospect Park

John F. Kennedy International Airport

STATEN ISLAND

BROOKLYN

Jamaica Bay

STATEN ISLAND

Lower New York Bay

Coney Island

Atlantic Beach

ATLANTIC OCEAN

0   4   8 km

0   4 miles

Gateway to America

New York was and is still regarded by many as the main entry point to the USA. The Statue of Liberty stands in New York harbor to remind people that the United States is a country of immigrants. Many have remained close to where they or their parents landed in New York harbor. The wide diversity of neighborhoods within the city reflects its many different races and cultures. In the city there are significant communities of Italians, Koreans, Chinese, and Russians, to name but a few. This mix of peoples creates the feeling of vibrancy in the city as each group contributes its foods, dress style, and customs.

A working city

New York began as a trading port. In this role it attracted service industries like banking and insurance, and this was the beginning of New York's hugely important financial industry. The Financial District around Wall Street is one of the most important in the world. The headquarters of many international businesses and organizations, including the United Nations, are located in New York because it is an international trade hub.

▲ The Statue of Liberty, given by France in 1886, is seen around the world as a symbol of freedom.

A city of many varied attractions

Visitors come to New York for many reasons. Some arrive on business, some for shopping, and others for the cultural attractions—to experience the city's special mix of history, culture, theater, and shopping. It has many museums and galleries, including the Guggenheim Museum on Fifth Avenue and the National Museum of the American Indian. There are green spaces such as Central Park where people can relax. Boat tours and ferries ply the East and Hudson Rivers, giving a completely different view of the city from the water. There are many street parades and celebrations representing the huge cultural diversity of the city's population.

◄ The Brooklyn Bridge, completed in 1883, is regarded as one of the industrial wonders of the world.

The history of New York

Native Americans were living on Manhattan Island 11,000 years before Europeans came to America. The island was called Manahatouh, which means a place for gathering wood for bows. There was an ancient path that crossed the island diagonally, which is now the route taken by Broadway. On the City Seal is a representation of the original inhabitants of Manhattan Island, standing to the right of the central shield.

▲ The City Seal has been used since the 17th century and includes several elements of the city's history, such as the beavers representing the early fur trade. The Latin inscription says, "Seal of the City of New York."

◀ Liberty Island, home to the Statue of Liberty, is a popular destination for tourists visiting New York.

The coming of the Europeans

The first Europeans to settle the area were the Dutch, who called the whole region New Netherlands and the new settlement New Amsterdam. The City Seal, which is still used today, features a shield with the sails of a Dutch windmill, showing the Dutch origins of the city. Flour and beaver pelts were two important early exports. The main markets for these products were in Europe, so a large merchant fleet was soon established in the port, and sailors' families formed a large part of the population. In 1664 the city was taken over by the English and renamed New York.

The growing city

In 1781 the American War of Independence gave the colonies of North America independence from Great Britain. In that year the population of New York City was 33,000. The chance of jobs and a better life attracted people from within America and from countries overseas as distant as Scotland, Ireland, and Germany. The 19th century was a period of rapid urbanization, and housing had to be built for these new Americans. By 1830 the population had risen to 250,000.

In 1825 New York was linked to the Great Lakes and the interior of the United States by the building of the Erie Canal, which connected with the Hudson River. More trade was then sent through New York's port, creating more jobs and attracting even more people. By 1850 the population was 515,547, making New York the second-largest city in the world. This growth was the impetus for the creation of the other boroughs of the city.

By the beginning of the 20th century the first skyscrapers were being built, which were to give New York its distinctive skyline. Rapid urbanization continued and by 1930 the population was 7 million. Just before this date, in 1929, there was a huge financial disaster when the stock market on Wall Street (at the southern end of Manhattan) crashed. Many firms went out of business and millions of people lost all of their money. This was the start of a period known as the Great Depression. Huge numbers of people were left unemployed across America and much of the world. The Depression only ended with the start of World War II in Europe, in 1939.

▶ The 285-foot-high Flatiron building was the tallest building in the world when it was built in 1902. Its steel-frame construction and the invention of elevators made its height possible.

The Forties and Fifties

New York was undamaged by World War II. After the war the new United Nations organization was set up there in 1946, and the city's importance as a financial center grew as the U.S. economy expanded. During the 1940s and 1950s more middle-class people moved into the suburbs to escape the problems associated with city living—high levels of crime, pollution, and poor city services. At the same time the manufacturing industry was slowing and service industries did not immediately replace it. The TV and film industry completed its move to Los Angeles, California. The city began to decline.

▼ Moving to the outer boroughs, such as here on Staten Island, New Yorkers could enjoy more space.

The Sixties and Seventies

These were unhappy years for New York. Racial tensions exploded into riots in Harlem, caused largely by poor living conditions and unemployment during hot summers. City services were poorly run and maintained, and the middle class continued to leave the central city. This slow decay reached its lowest point in 1975, when the city was on the verge of bankruptcy. New York was only saved with a huge loan from the U.S. government. The completion of the World Trade Center in the mid-1970s coincided with the emergence of a healthier economy.

▼ The Twin Towers of the World Trade Center became a symbol of the rebirth of the city. They were destroyed by terrorists in 2001.

Into the 21st century

The 1980s began well for New York—businesses flourished and property prices rose rapidly—but this period of growth ended with another stock market crash in 1987. This crash was a serious setback for the city's financial businesses. After a slow recovery the 1990s were marked by the policies of the administration of Mayor Rudolph Giuliani. He took a no-nonsense stand on crime and worked to clean up many areas of the city.

On September 11, 2001, the Twin Towers of the World Trade Center were destroyed when terrorists crashed two airplanes into them. For a while both business transactions and tourism were reduced. On July 4, 2004, builders laid the cornerstone of the Freedom Tower, which is to replace the Twin Towers and reach some 400 feet higher within the Manhattan skyline. Since then the city's economy has recovered, and although the gap between rich and poor

▲ The site of the Twin Towers is now known as Ground Zero. Work has started on a replacement tower, designed by the architect Daniel Liebeskind.

seems to be widening, the quality of life for the majority of New Yorkers is improving overall. Many former industrial areas are being redeveloped as new housing, green space, or business locations, and New York is looking to provide all of its inhabitants with the means to enjoy a city life.

CASE STUDY

Firefighter Kevin Erdman

Kevin has been a firefighter for more than 20 years. "New York City has always been a difficult city to fight fires in," he says. "Any modern city with this many high-rise buildings and skyscrapers has to be hard: Ladders are only so long! So our challenge as firefighters has to be one of prevention and not cure." Kevin lost five friends in the terrorist attack of September 11, 2001. "No fire service could have better dealt with the tragedy of 9/11. We did our best and lost some of the best doing our job but we saved lives, lots of lives." He wants to see the Twin Towers site developed as a memorial to those who died.

The people of New York

Early European settlement of the city of New York began with the Dutch and the English, but these nationalities were soon joined by people from many other countries. New York's position as the premier port of the United States meant it was the main point of entry for most migrants up until the latter part of the 20th century. Many immigrants settled in the city through which they entered the country.

▲ There is a very broad range of ethnic backgrounds among New Yorkers, including European, Afro-Caribbean, and Chinese.

Up until the 19th century most immigrants were from western and northern Europe. In the 1840s there was a huge surge in Irish immigration, driven by the impact of the severe famines caused by the failure of the potato crop. The 19th century also saw large numbers of Jews migrating to avoid persecution in eastern Europe and Russia. From 1870 to 1930 Italians also formed an important immigrant group. By 1890 42 percent of the population of New York City was European-born.

All of these peoples crowded into the city, often living in very cramped and unhealthy conditions, frequently with a family of six or seven living in one room. The pressure caused by a continuous flow of people meant that the city grew outward, and those with some money left the crowded areas on Manhattan Island and moved to the new suburbs of Brooklyn, Queens, and the Bronx. Many immigrants to New York and America came through the Ellis Island Immigration Station (opened in 1892); it is estimated that before it closed in 1954, 12 million people had passed through. On arrival immigrants were given health checks, and those who had infectious diseases were sent back to their countries of origin.

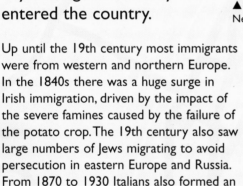

◀ The population growth of the New York metropolitan area from 1950 onward.

Expansion

Today the city continues to grow as it attracts migrants from abroad. New immigrants are now more likely to come from Asia than Europe. More than a third of all New Yorkers are now first-generation immigrants, a figure unmatched since the last great wave of immigration between 1880 and 1920. Some find well-paid positions, but most newcomers from abroad find low-paid jobs. New York also attracts people from within the United States, because it offers a stimulating environment for people with new ideas in many different fields, from technology to the arts. But the growth of the city has led to problems in transportation, housing, and air and noise pollution, as well as water supply and waste disposal.

▲ African Americans have formed part of New York's population from colonial times.

▲ Traffic congestion is a major problem for the city, as more and more vehicles try to use an outdated road system.

The neighborhoods

People refer to New York as a city of neighborhoods—there are many distinctive areas within the city. These vary according to the ethnic background and culture of the residents. Each group of migrants that entered the city tended to look for people who were from the same culture and spoke the same language. They needed someone who could explain what was expected of them as new citizens in the city, where they could find familiar foods, and how they could get employment. There is a Little Italy, Little India, and Little Korea. The Jewish area was originally situated around the Lower East Side and there are still Jewish businesses and synagogues in this area. Today many of the Jews have moved out to more spacious neighborhoods in Brooklyn, and their place has been taken by the expansion of Chinatown. Chinatown is an old and distinctive district with its specialized shops, markets, restaurants, and temples. When a neighborhood has a clearly defined geographical boundary and within it there is a concentration of people of a similar ethnic or cultural background, it is sometimes called a ghetto.

▼ Orthodox Jewish men on the Lower East Side.

Racial structure of the boroughs by percentage					
Borough	White	Hispanic	Black	Asian	Other
Bronx	14.5	48.4	31.2	2.9	3
Brooklyn	34.7	19.8	34.4	7.5	3.6
Manhattan	45.8	27.2	15.3	9.4	2.3
Queens	32.9	25	19	17.5	5.6
Staten Island	71.3	12.1	8.9	5.6	2.1

Source: Adapted from U.S. Census 2000

Harlem

Harlem stretches north from the top of Central Park up to 140th Street and is historically the most important African-American residential district in New York. Originally an area of country estates, it was developed for the middle class after the coming of the subway at the start of the 20th century. When not enough whites were willing to move that far uptown, the houses were subdivided and rented to African Americans.

Harlem developed a distinctive black culture with jazz and blues clubs, soul food restaurants, and shops. Lack of maintenance of much of the housing, poor schools, and high crime and unemployment rates spelled decline for the neighborhood. By the end of the 1970s there had been a 30 percent decline in the population as families left for the suburbs. Today, with its desirable brownstone houses and easy access to midtown Manhattan, Harlem is attracting a wide range of people of all ethnic backgrounds. African Americans still make up more than three quarters of the population. Young professionals are buying

▲ Traditional brownstone houses in Harlem.

up the old houses and renovating the interiors (the exteriors are protected by law). This is having a positive impact on the urban environment but it means that Harlem natives are finding it harder to afford housing where they were brought up.

CASE STUDY

Harlem resident Elenor Watson

Elenor originally came from Belize and has lived in Harlem for 10 years. She is a single mother of two teenage boys and works as a street cleaner. "Harlem used to be thought of as a 'black only' suburb but now it's becoming a very trendy place to live. Young professionals from lower Manhattan are buying up all the houses and putting security gates on them. The area isn't as friendly now and people no longer sit on the steps to talk about their day. Developers want to buy up where I live and fill it with city types, but I like it here."

▲ Graduates from a language school celebrate finishing their course.

The newest New Yorkers

In 2000 2.9 million people, or 36 percent of the population of the city of New York, were foreign-born. Nearly a quarter of the foreign-born were from the continent of Asia and nearly a third were from Latin America. In 1970 two thirds of the foreign-born residents were from Europe, but 20 years later the largest source country was the Dominican Republic in the Caribbean: 369,000 migrants arrived during the 1990s. China provided 262,000 migrants during the same period. Without immigrants New York would be losing population. From 1990 to 2000 475,000 people left the city for other U.S. states. During the same period 339,000 foreign immigrants entered the city, providing a stable population base. Because the new immigrants tend to be in the younger age bands, mainly 24–35, they are also at the age when they have children. Such births raise the city's birthrate and help maintain the population level.

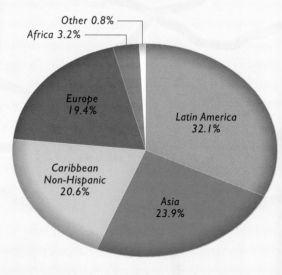

Other 0.8%
Africa 3.2%
Europe 19.4%
Latin America 32.1%
Caribbean Non-Hispanic 20.6%
Asia 23.9%

▲ Origin of recent immigrants to New York.

Settling in

Of the new migrants, 69 percent made their home in the largely residential areas of Queens and Brooklyn. The immigrants from the Dominican Republic, however, tended to settle in northern Manhattan or the southwest Bronx, where there is a well established neighborhood of Dominicans. As a result of immigrants settling in areas where there are already people from their cultures, many ethnic residential neighborhoods are growing outward.

New York City needs immigrants to work in many areas, but these newcomers are found mainly in the manufacturing, construction, and service industries. Those who already have some knowledge of English tend to settle in fastest. For people who lack English skills there are many free courses where immigrants are encouraged to learn English as part of their commitment to citizenship in their new country. Many schools in New York run special intensive language classes for children of immigrants who have come to the United States without any English skills. Some schools specialize in teaching children who have never been to school in any country. These schools teach children in a bilingual environment to encourage learning as well as language skills.

In addition, many volunteer groups in the city help new immigrants to find housing and employment. Some government help is also available, especially for those who are seeking asylum from persecution in their own countries.

CASE STUDY

Phyllis Berman

Phyllis is a director of the Riverside Language Program in New York, an institution that runs free intensive English courses for new migrants to the city. Sixty percent of students come with no or very little English. They attend the course for six weeks and then take an oral English examination. The origins of the students are constantly changing. "At present a third of our students are from Russia, a third from Latin American countries, and the remainder are from the rest of the world. At a recent registration for new students we saw people who spoke Russian, Albanian, Romanian, Polish, Bosnian, French, Spanish, Portuguese, Chinese, Japanese, Korean, Tibetan, Italian, German, Mali, Hebrew, Arabic, and some tribal languages!"

◄ Working in her office in the Upper West Side, Phyllis Berman has been overseeing English language courses for new immigrants for 26 years.

Living in the city

New York is a city of contrasts. The noise and congestion of traffic on Fifth Avenue gives way within a block or two to the calm oasis of greenery that is Central Park. There are busy waterfronts in Brooklyn and Manhattan close to theatrical and cultural venues. Upscale stores are found in central Manhattan and yet not too far away are shops selling ancient Chinese herbal remedies and Asian foods.

Urbanization

Manhattan is the heart of the city, but it is an island and space is restricted. Even in the 19th century tall, narrow houses were built to make the most of the space. Early apartment buildings called tenements were built in the poorer areas. In the 19th century these were very crowded and poorly ventilated, and clusters of tenements were often areas where crime flourished. One such area, in today's Chelsea and the Garment District, was known as Hell's Kitchen, and many criminal gangs were based here. On the very expensive central land the skyscraper was developed. In 1902 the 285-foot Flatiron building was built (see page 13); it was so tall people thought it would fall over. This compares with the now destroyed World Trade Center, built in 1977 at 1,368 feet high. The farther out from Manhattan you travel, the more residential housing there is and the more likely it is to be low rise.

▲ Skyscraper offices and homes make the most of small plots of expensive land in the center of the city.

Wealth and poverty

While the United States is the richest country in the world, there are still poor people. But even the poor are well off relative to standards of living around the world. There are public housing developments (usually apartment buildings) for those with low incomes. Many poor families depend on money from the city. In 2002 nearly half a million people were receiving public assistance, but in New York people who are able to work have to work for some of their welfare payments under a program called "Workfare." The goal is for participants to gain work experience and get some training that can help them to find a job.

▼ Large public housing projects are home to many of the city's poorer residents.

Health

Americans need to have private medical insurance to cover medical bills when they fall ill. The poorest families cannot afford this but have basic medical coverage through a government program called Medicaid. Good jobs often provide family medical insurance as part of employment benefits. People with private insurance are more likely to be able to access the city's very high quality private hospitals.

Poor northwest area of Queens contrasted with wealthy Upper East Side of Manhattan.
(Department of City Planning, 2002)

	QUEENS	MANHATTAN
Birthrate (per 1,000)	9.9	12.8
Death rate (per 1,000)	7.4	6.6
Infant mortality	2.5	2.2
% on Medicaid	19.5	4.5
% White non-Hispanic	41	83
% Asian	36	6
% Hispanic	17	6
% Population less than 18 years	20	12
% Unemployed	5.3	3.7
% Single-family dwellings	34	5
% Multifamily dwellings	10	35
Average income	$46,294	$87,428

Education

In New York, school officially begins at age six in the first grade. Before that many children attend day care centers or kindergarten. The school population reflects the mix of races and cultures in the city, and many primary schools have children with Caribbean, Asian, European, and Hispanic origins. In New York City there are some schools that work particularly with the children of newly arrived immigrants, such as the Liberty School in Manhattan. It provides a high school environment for non-English-speaking immigrants, teaching English to the students while offering cultural and artistic activities in their first languages, such as Chinese, Spanish, and Polish. Some high schools are specialized academies, each with a curriculum that focuses on one area, such as performing arts, science, or mathematics.

Some New York City schools have had severe problems with violence and weapon carrying. The number of violent incidents has fallen since the early 1990s, however. School security has been significantly tightened, and today anyone found carrying a weapon in school is immediately expelled. Security guards equipped with metal detectors operate at some school entrances to check students for weapons as they arrive.

New York is home to several universities, including three that are of world importance: New York University (NYU), Cornell, and Columbia.

▼ The Low Memorial Library forms a focal point on the main square of Columbia University.

Shopping

Shopping is an important activity for both residents and visitors, and there is a huge range of outlets within the city. Fifth Avenue is home to many stores selling expensive clothes and accessories. Another important shopping area is Rockefeller Center in midtown Manhattan. Today it has many shops, offices, and entertainment venues, as well as gardens to walk in. Bloomingdale's and Macy's are both famous department stores—Macy's is the largest in the world, taking over a whole city block, where you can buy anything from a potato peeler to jewelery.

Small grocery stores and supermarkets are common, providing items for particular ethnic neighborhoods. In Chinatown, Chinese markets sell live seafood as well as Asian vegetables. The "green markets" are another shopping attraction, where New York State farmers come in to sell fresh fruit, vegetables, and other produce such as honey. These markets, with their fresh and often organically produced foods, are very popular with local residents.

▲ The clothes in this dress shop are likely to have been made locally within the Garment District of New York.

▶ Macy's is one of several very large department stores in New York.

Hot and cold

New York has huge contrasts in its climate. Its residents need to use air conditioning units in the summer to cope with hot and humid conditions yet must use central heating to cope with freezing winter temperatures. The city structure of concrete, stone, and asphalt holds heat and the high buildings deflect winds, so the city temperature is usually a few degrees warmer than the surrounding countryside. Extreme weather events can still bring the city to a standstill. In February 2006 a storm caused a 27-inch blanket of snow. All flights from the three airports were canceled. Temperatures dropped to 5°F and many schools and offices were closed.

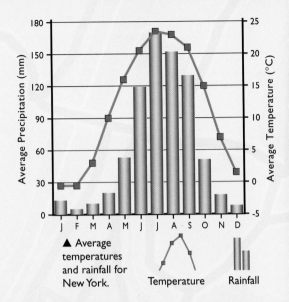

▲ Average temperatures and rainfall for New York.

Temperature   Rainfall

Noise, pests, and trash

Noise is the number one complaint to the city's Citizen Service Center. New York is one of the noisiest cities in the world. The noise comes from loud music, car alarms, traffic, the constant road works, and aircraft, but the main offenders are noisy neighbors, a problem especially hard to escape in Manhattan, where people live in very close proximity to one another.

New York produces more than 12,000 tons of trash every day. Apart from the problem of getting rid of it is the problem of the pests that the stored garbage attracts, especially rats. Pest control officers are continually working to get rid of infestations and encourage people to store their waste in rodent-proof containers. As well as rats, many residents constantly have to battle with cockroaches.

◀ Freezing winters are followed by sweltering summers. These children cool down in a fountain in a neighborhood park.

Homelessness

Like many other cities, New York has thousands of homeless people. Some are homeless because they have lost their jobs or because they are recent immigrants. Others are homeless because of problems with drugs, alcohol, or mental health. In March 2005 there were nearly 36,000 homeless people, including children, in emergency housing.

Crime

The New York City Police Department (NYPD) has the difficult job of policing this vast and multicultural city. It has foot, car, and mounted police patrols and in June 2005 had about 35,000 officers. Since 1993 the number and severity of crime incidents have declined, and the department is looking to prevent crime from happening rather than dealing with its effects. The

▲ Many homeless people can be seen on the streets.

Crime Prevention Section of the NYPD carries out security surveys for residents and gives lectures on crime issues. It also helps residents to security mark their property so it can be returned if found after a burglary. The NYPD organizes a variety of programs to help stop car and bike theft within the city and provides a range of crime-prevention literature.

NYPD Crime Statistics, 1993 vs. 2004

	in 2004	% change
Murder	572	−70.3
Rape	1,741	−46.0
Robbery	24,124	−71.9
Assault	18,186	−55.7
Burglary	26,815	−73.4
Grand larceny	48,361	−43.5
Car theft	20,288	−81.8

◀ Tourist areas are policed by foot patrols.

The New York economy

Unemployment levels are low in New York City—in 2005 the rate was 5.3 percent. But many jobs are in the service sector, and these may be low paid.

Poorer New Yorkers may have to hold down two jobs to be able to survive in the city. Although today most of New York's residents are employed within the services sector (including jobs in education, finance, retailing, transportation, and administration), this has been a relatively recent change. The city grew on trade with Europe and beyond —an early example of globalization—and many of its early industries were based on the goods that went through the port, such as sugar refining. Later in the 19th century heavy industries, such as metalworking and other forms of manufacturing, played an important role. As these heavy industries were thriving, service industries such as banking and finance were developing to support them. These service industries now dominate New York's economy. Manufacturing industries have largely moved over the Hudson River into New Jersey or out to the suburbs, where there is room for modern factories and the land is cheaper. The southern end of Manhattan, which was once an important area for manufacturing and port industries, is now the main financial district of the city. It can be recognized by the cluster of very tall skyscrapers. Some old industries such as garment manufacture have managed to remain in Manhattan, even though the original reasons for the location have disappeared. The area has a skilled labor force and a successful fashion industry has developed there now.

▲ Skilled workers continue to make clothing in the Garment District, in Manhattan, for the fashion industry.

▶ Major fashion brands based in New York include Donna Karan, Marc Jacobs, and Ralph Lauren. This fashion designer works as one of a team of designers at Donna Karan, a major label that was started in New York in 1984, based in the Garment District.

Primary Industry 4.4%

Manufacturing 6.6%

Services
89%

▲ Areas of employment in New York City.

Fulton Fish Market

The Fulton Fish Market was founded in 1821 in lower Manhattan, located near the South Street Seaport. It was a popular sight for visitors, and local people enjoyed being able to buy freshly caught fish every morning. Even though the market was near the port, fish no longer comes in directly from boats but by truck from fishing docks elsewhere. It is difficult to drive delivery trucks across Manhattan because of traffic congestion, so in July 2005 the market moved to Hunts Point in the Bronx. Although not popular with traditionalists, the move has brought much better road and rail access and the market is in a custom-built facility that meets modern high safety and hygiene standards.

◀ Most of the fish in Fulton Fish Market is sold before dawn!

CASE STUDY

Anthony Bencivenga, fish wholesaler

Anthony is 62 years old and was one of the longest-working fishmongers in the Fulton Street Market. He began work at 14 and now employs 40 people, importing fish from all over the world. He lives outside the city and welcomed the opportunity to move his business to Hunts Point. "At Fulton Street this is no way to run a multimillion-dollar industry. Nothing has changed here for 200 years. The move to Hunts Point will cost us more but it's clean, spacious, and above all it's environmentally hygienic."

Banking and finance

New York City is the financial center of the United States and one of the three biggest financial centers in the global economy. The New York Stock Exchange (NYSE) and headquarters of many national banks and insurance companies are located in the Financial District around Wall Street in southern Manhattan, near the Hudson River. NYSE is one of the busiest and most eagerly watched stock exchanges in the world, with the shares of more than 2,000 companies being traded. The presence of such an important financial center attracts other businesses to the city, which want to be close to the place where decisions are made.

▶ The statue of George Washington, standing in front of Federal Hall, looks toward the front of the New York Stock Exchange, in the heart of the Financial District.

Advertising and the media

Many advertising firms are located in New York to be close to the great range of businesses that require their services. Some are small Web-based firms, but others provide the advertising needed by large international companies. Being located in an appealing and exciting city also attracts young advertising executives with new ideas for marketing products.

There are many large book publishers located in New York, including Scholastic, the largest publisher and distributor of children's books in the United States. There are also several national newspapers produced in the city, including the *Wall Street Journal*, which is a daily financial publication, and the prestigious *New York Times*. A range of magazines are produced, including *Newsweek*, a weekly summary of national and international news.

With more than 145 studios and stages in the city, New York is becoming ever more popular as a film and television location, rivaling the huge industry of Los Angeles. Films and shows made in the city are shown around the world. There are many local drama schools and colleges of performing arts that provide a steady supply of young actors looking for work.

▲ Times Square, in midtown Manhattan, is famous for its brightly lit advertising.

CASE STUDY

Lisa Gallagher, Publisher

Lisa is Publisher of William Morrow, part of HarperCollins in New York. New York is the hub of book publishing in the United States, with hundreds of publishing companies of all sizes employing tens of thousands of people. Lisa, who has worked in publishing in New York since 1998, says, "Being in New York puts a publisher at the center of the dynamic artistic and cultural capital of the country, which helps us to produce the books we think will appeal to the reading public."

High-tech industries

There are more than 4,000 technology and media companies in New York. Originally most of these firms were located in lower Manhattan. Over the last 10 years these firms, including telecommunications and information technology companies, have moved to northern Manhattan, Queens, and Brooklyn. The companies want to be in New York City for the easy access to possible investors and to be close to world-class universities, their research departments, and a pool of well-qualified graduates. High-technology firms also tend to cluster together, because this allows an exchange of ideas and faster development. The city location helps companies retain workers because it offers a potentially better quality of life. New York State wants to encourage high-tech industries, which are providing a range of new jobs.

▲ Tourists, here on a sightseeing bus, provide an important part of the city's income.

Tourism

Tourism is a very important service industry for New York. In 2004 there were 40 million visitors to the city. While there they spent more than $15 billion and supported more than a quarter million jobs. These service jobs include city guides, hotel workers, tour operators, and waiters. The people employed had money to spend within the city economy too, further contributing to the city. Now that air travel is cheaper, New York is no longer the once-in-a-lifetime destination it once was for foreign visitors. People from Europe now visit the city for a few days just to do their Christmas shopping or to visit the sales in the big department stores. Although temperatures can be freezing in winter there is much to see that is under cover, and New York is now an all-year-round destination.

Marketing the city

NYC & Company is New York's official tourism marketing organization. It provides information and assistance to business and tourists via the web, pamphlets, and ads in various journals. It also helps to publicize activities to help the many tourist-dependent businesses get as many people as possible to come to stay in and enjoy the city—and spend lots of money!

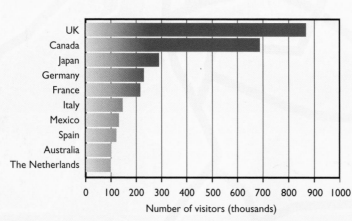

◀ The top ten countries providing international tourist visitors to New York (2003).

Number of visitors (thousands)

A safe destination

Because its crime rates have seen a steady and significant reduction since 1993, New York is now the safest of the large cities of the United States. Daytime travel on public transportation is safe and cheap, and it is used by large numbers of tourists.

New York wants to continue to increase its numbers of visitors, especially from overseas. One initiative the city has helped organize is CultureFest, a showcase of arts and cultural organizations that now occurs annually in Battery Park, right at the southern tip of Manhattan.

▶ The entrance lobby of the Empire State Building, perhaps New York's most famous building. Tourists can ascend to the top of the building to take in the famous Manhattan skyline.

▼ A horse-drawn carriage takes visitors on a leisurely tour of Central Park.

Regeneration

Once industry or activity moves out of an area, there is often a need to restore and redevelop the locality so that it can be sustained as a productive area. It may be changed into a residential area, an area of light industry, a tourist site, a green space, or a mix of all these. Land that has stopped serving one use is transformed to the benefit of the local community.

South Street Seaport

This waterfront area in the southeast of Manhattan was the heart of the early 19th-century port. When sailing ships dominated, it was a bustling area of warehouses and inns, and South Street was known as "The Street of Ships." During the second half of the 19th century, however, this port area began to decline as heavier and larger steamships migrated to the deeper waters of the Hudson River, on the west side of Manhattan. By the mid-20th century the Fulton Fish Market was the only remaining part of its port industries, and the area was looking very rundown. During the 1960s planners decided to restore and redevelop the area. Part of

▲ Buildings in the South Street Seaport area awaiting redevelopment.

the seaport area has been pedestrianized so that visitors can escape from the usual New York traffic. The historic buildings now house restaurants, craft shops, and the South Street Seaport Museum. Pier 17 was redeveloped in 1982 and now has a pavilion made of glass and steel. This has three floors housing stores, food stalls, and restaurants. The top floor has views of the Brooklyn Bridge and New York Harbor. Visitors now come to take in the views, to eat, and to enjoy the craft demonstrations and stores. Workers from the nearby Financial District eat lunch here on a daily basis and the port has become a lively area once again.

◄ The South Street Seaport has been restored to provide a range of retail and eating outlets and is popular with locals.

▲ A view of South Street Seaport, in lower Manhattan, from the East River.

Brooklyn waterfront

Although there is still some maritime use of the Brooklyn waterfront, much of the area has derelict buildings, such as old sugar refineries and warehouses. The Brooklyn Navy Yard, which closed in 1966, has started to be redeveloped. It is a large site with good views of Manhattan. One of the first developments was Steiner Studios, which opened in 2004. The studios have stages, offices, and dressing rooms, plus a 100-seat room for showing films. Light industries and offices are being attracted into the secure Navy site.

Other developments planned for Brooklyn include building over the railyards. The goal is to replace a rundown area with a new, mixed-use complex of buildings, including a sports stadium, low- and middle-income housing, open recreation space, and offices.

Managing New York

Although New York City is in New York State and comes under that state's laws, it has considerable powers of its own through its City Council.

▲ City Hall, built in the early 19th century, is the seat of government for New York City.

The government of the city has three branches: executive (overseeing the departments that run the day-to-day activities of the city); legislative (creating laws for the city); and judicial (the work of the civil court of the city). The City Council is composed of 51 members from the 51 Council Districts that make up the City of New York. Each member represents the views of about 157,000 people. The City Council is the body that can make laws for the city, and it decides how much can be spent and on what within the city. The council checks how various city departments are performing, and its members sit on committees linked to the

departments. The head of the City Council is the Speaker, who is elected by the council members. Her main job is to get an overall agreement on major issues from council members. New York City's government is led by the mayor, who is elected by the citizens every four years. In 2002 Michael Bloomberg became the 108th Mayor of the City of New York. He is aided by five deputy mayors. The mayor has to approve decisions made by the council. If he disagrees with a decision the matter is returned to the council for reconsideration. If it then receives a clear majority, however, the council can override the mayor's decision.

Departments

There are a number of city departments covering areas such as transportation and parks. These departments carry out the work approved by the City Council. The Department of Environmental Protection has more than 5,700 people working for it. It protects watercourses from pollution, ensures a good-quality drinking water supply, and works to improve air quallity.

The Department of Youth and Community Development provides information for youth and community groups, funds neighborhood outreach and youth activities, and develops programs of youth work.

▶ The Department of Health battles the city's rat infestation.

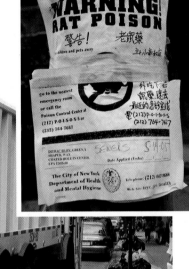

▲ Much of the city's waste goes to landfill sites in other states.

◀ City traffic officers are needed to keep the traffic moving.

Committees

Each City Council member usually sits on about three committees which oversee the various functions of city government. The results of committee meetings can be accessed online so New York citizens can see what is taking place in their government.

The Department of City Planning

This important department is responsible for making decisions about how land can be used or developed. It controls the zoning of land use so that, for example, industrial zones are kept separate from residential areas. The Department of City Planning has to resolve conflicts between industrial, residential, and transportation land uses, as well as planning for recreational space. Its goal is to ensure that any growth is sustainable and improves the landscapes of the city for all its citizens.

▲ A view of Manhattan showing the density of building on the island. New developments must be tightly controlled.

Planning conflicts

Throgs Neck is an area by the water in the Bronx where there is conflict between the residents and developers. The residents feel that the character of the area is being changed by the inappropriate development of tall, multifamily town houses along the waterfront. There was also a problem with a lack of parking for residents. The Planning Department has resolved the problem by rezoning Throgs Neck as a Lower Density Growth Management (LDGM) area. This gives priority to single-family houses built at a low density—houses with front, side, and back gardens.

New houses on the waterfront cannot be more than two stories high so they do not restrict views to the water, and there must be spaces between the individual houses. Widths of building plots have also been increased so that cars can be parked within the property boundary and not affect the character of the area. New waterfront houses must also have gardens to the front to improve the appearance of the area from the water. Rezoning has ensured that landowners know the rules set out by the Planning Department for any future developments.

Hudson Yards

As part of the development of the west side of Manhattan, the area known as Hudson Yards is to provide an extension of the island's central business area. The increased pressure of urbanization, as more companies locate their headquarters in New York and more workers are attracted to live in the city, means there is a need for more office and residential space to be built. This will help stop the movement out of the city to find adequate office space and will slow down urbanization at the edge of the city.

Hudson Yards is a 360-acre area, part of which consists of railroad tracks and yards. The Planning Department's ideas for the future include covering the railyards and allowing building on top. By 2012 the subway link and basic clearance would be completed. Private developers would then move in to build offices and homes.

▲ The underused area around the Hudson Yards is to be redeveloped to provide much-needed office and living space for west Manhattan.

CASE STUDY

Ryan Singer, city planner

Ryan came to New York from Seattle three years ago to work as a city planner. The city is changing so fast that it needs a long-term outlook. "Our job in the Planning Department is one of balancing the needs of developers and businesses, who want to expand, and residents, who want to live in a better environment. Environmental issues are important, and too many apartment buildings lead to more cars and then more air pollution. We are trying to build on more brownfield sites to reuse land in the city. Keeping new residential properties out of the sky—that is, more high-density, low-rise buildings—should lead to a cleaner and friendlier neighborhood for all of us—just like the old days!"

Transportation for New York

When New York was first settled it was a compact town, and people either walked or used horse-drawn vehicles such as carriages or carts. Gradually the island of Manhattan became too crowded and people settled the other boroughs. Commuting at the speed of a horse was slow, so people who came to the city often could not live very far away. In the early 20th century other types of transportation became possible and people could live much farther out. This led to increasing urban sprawl.

▲ Looking across Brooklyn Bridge (foreground) and Manhattan Bridge (rear) toward the borough of Brooklyn.

City center problems

Because Manhattan is an island, efficient transportation links have always been important. Today the island is linked to the other boroughs by 17 main bridges and four tunnels. The most famous is the Brooklyn Bridge, built in 1883, which links Brooklyn to Manhattan. During peak times the bridges and tunnels become very congested with car and truck traffic. In 2002 the U.S. Census Bureau calculated that the average time in a year New Yorkers spent commuting to work was 6.7 days, compared with 4.9 for Los Angeles. The city's government is trying, through a number of different initiatives, to reduce the number of cars entering Manhattan to improve both traffic flow and air quality.

▼ Heavy Manhattan-bound rush-hour traffic.

Railway and subway

Surface rail to Manhattan arrives at two main terminals. Commuter trains from the north suburbs come into Grand Central Station, and those from the east and west enter Pennsylvania Station, which also receives long-distance trains.

In 1904 the subway opened, and today the city has 468 stations. In 2002 the subway carried 4.8 million passengers per day, but the system needs updating. Recently computer-aided subway cars were introduced that give passengers information about arrival times. Besides being more technologically advanced than the old cars, they are also more environmentally friendly, with the heat energy created by braking being fed back into the power system.

▲ A section of the now disused High Line.

The High Line

In the 1930s freight train tracks were raised above the road level on the west side of Manhattan to reduce the number of street-level crossings and help avoid accidents. This was known as the High Line. Interstate trucking replaced its function, and trains stopped running on the track in 1980. It was neglected and became covered in wildflowers. Part of the High Line, however, is about to be restored into a green walkway, a sort of promenade above the street linking into the general development of that side of Manhattan. It will mean that people can walk for 22 blocks without using roads and have access to the waterfront regeneration area too.

Taking the bus

Buses began to carry passengers in the city in 1907. Today there are more than 200 local routes and 4,500 buses. The city is moving toward greener, more sustainable transportation and now has more than 6,000 buses running on alternative fuels such as compressed natural gas (CNG), electricity, and biofuel (a fuel made from plants). Some buses run on a mixture of low sulfur diesel and electric motors. The two combine to run economically with far lower emissions than standard buses. The goal of New York City Transit, which operates the buses and subways, is to provide efficient service while improving air quality.

▲ Many of the city's 4,500 blue and white buses run on a 24-hour schedule.

◀ ▼ The subway is a quick and inexpensive way to travel around New York, but it can become very crowded at peak times.

Airports

New York has three airports. The main international airport is John F. Kennedy (JFK), which is in southeast Queens, about 16 miles away from midtown Manhattan. In 2002 it dealt with 35 million passengers. The second international airport is Newark Liberty International, which is also about 16 miles away. It has easy access to Manhattan by train but people tend to think it is farther away because it is in another state, New Jersey. The third airport is La Guardia, which is 9 miles away from midtown Manhattan in northwest Queens. This is mainly a domestic airport, because it cannot take wide-bodied jets. The links between the airports and the center of the city have been improved, with dedicated train and bus services offering a fast and reasonably priced alternative to driving and parking a car. These services also reduce traffic congestion and exhaust emissions on the approach roads.

Shipping

It is easy to forget that New York is still an important port. Although much of the commercial shipping has moved across the Hudson to better sites in New Jersey, New York still shares management via the Port Authority of New York and Jew Jersey. Manhattan is an important port of call for cruise liners. The New York Cruise Terminal is being upgraded to cope with the increasing number of visitors who arrive by ship. A new cruise terminal is also being developed in Brooklyn, the first part of which opened in 2005. Ferries are an everyday feature of the New York Harbor. The most famous is the free service from Manhattan to Staten Island, which is heavily used by both commuters and tourists. These and many others ferry services allow commuters to leave their cars outside the central city.

▼ The free Staten Island ferry runs to and from Manhattan 24 hours a day.

CASE STUDY

Charlie Ventycinque, taxi driver

Charlie came from Italy with his parents when he was eight, and he has never returned. He works as a taxi driver on Staten Island. "Life on Staten Island is fine. I'd hate to have to deal with the rush and push over on Manhattan. I avoid going there like the plague. Now that the new ferry terminal has been built there are even more commuters living over here and working in the city. It's safer living over here, and if they can afford the property prices— good luck to them. It means more business for me, too!"

Culture, leisure, and tourism

New York has an enormous range of cultural and leisure attractions, with world-famous museums, art galleries, theaters and a glittering and energetic nightlife. It has a huge range of parks and open spaces.

Central Park

The most famous of all of the city's parks is Central Park in Manhattan. It was planned in 1858 to be the backyard (or garden) for all New Yorkers without access to their own green space. The 843-acre site was previously a mixture of swamps, piggeries, and quarries but today is a magnificent open space with lakes, hills, and meadows. It has roads across it but cars are banned on weekends to make the area safer and more pleasant. On a summer's day thousands of New

▲ This scene from *Alice in Wonderland*, made of bronze, is a popular spot for children in Central Park.

Yorkers can be seen enjoying the sun on the open lawns or sitting by the more formal gardens. There are also basketball and volleyball courts for rent, and they are well used. On the paths around the park are joggers and many Rollerbladers, but probably the best way to see this huge park is to ride a bicycle.

▲ In the heat of the summer Central Park offers shaded paths for those walking or just sitting on a bench.

Other open spaces

Other parks are dotted all over the city, giving the residents the chance for a view of sky and some greenery. Battery Park is located at the southern end of Manhattan and gives excellent views of the ocean. There are other parks around the edge of Manhattan as well as some smaller ones within it. The present mayor of New York,

Michael Bloomberg, has stated that he would like to see a recreational path around all of Manhattan for the use of residents for walking, playing, or generally relaxing. Prospect Park, in Brooklyn, is another large park created in the 19th century to offer recreational space to residents who lived in the new suburbs.

The Bronx is home to both the world-class Bronx Zoo and the New York Botanical Garden. The zoo specializes in the breeding of endangered species such as the lowland gorilla and has created exhibits that do away with traditional cages and bars. Moats and deep

ditches are used to separate people and animals. This is a popular day trip for New Yorkers, especially on Wednesdays when entry is via voluntary donation. The Botanical Garden was created at the end of the 19th century and is set in 250 acres of land. The huge greenhouses have desert and tropical habitats within them.

▶ A gorilla in the Bronx Zoo.

CASE STUDY

Bingo Wyer, Central Park volunteer

Bingo works as a writer for New York–based papers and magazines, but in her spare time she works as a volunteer in Central Park. "I've worked as a volunteer in Central Park for just two months. We work in small groups of about ten people, clearing leaves or pruning back trees and bushes—generally making the place tidy. We operate under the supervision of a paid Park Ranger who works full time for the New York Parks Department. The volunteers have been going for 25 years and it's just one more way we New Yorkers can put a little back into our own community and make our Central Park even more special."

45

The theater and the arts

New York City offers residents and visitors alike a huge range of venues for theater, concerts, and dance. In 1883 the Metropolitan Opera House opened on Broadway. This encouraged other theaters, restaurants and hotels to locate there. Today, the Theater District is still located in this area, mostly west of Broadway between 42nd and 53rd Streets. Well-known plays are said to be "on Broadway" and those less well known or more experimental appear "off Broadway." Later, with the advent of film, large movie theaters were developed in the same area. By the 1920s there were so many neon lights outside the various Broadway venues that the street became known as the "Great White Way." Times Square is at the heart of the Theater District and many visitors go there just to look at all the neon lights of the theaters and advertisers.

Besides the traditional theaters is a range of other venues such as the Performing Garage, where visitors can see experimental theater. Shakespeare in the Park is a summer event in which plays are performed in the open air in Central Park. Alternatively there is Shakespeare in the Park(ing Lot), another free event but taking place in a parking lot in Manhattan! New York has five ballet companies as well as many venues for seeing contemporary dance. The Brooklyn Academy of Music is an important dance venue and hosts the annual DanceAfrica Festival.

Carnegie Hall is a world-famous concert hall located just south of Central Park. Once home to the New York Philharmonic, it hosts important orchestras from around the world. The Philharmonic now plays a few blocks away at Lincoln Center. It gives free concerts in city parks in the summer, which many thousands of New Yorkers attend.

▼ Broadway is at the heart of New York's theater district and offers a wide variety of entertainment.

Museums and galleries

New York is home to many important art galleries and museums as well as to smaller, specialized collections. There are more than 60 museums in Manhattan alone. The Museum of Modern Art (MoMA) houses one of the largest and most important collections of modern art in the world. It shows paintings, sculpture, books, film, and design. Another museum displaying modern art is the Guggenheim Museum. It is not just the collection that is important, but also the building that contains it, which was designed by the architect Frank Lloyd Wright. It has a curving shape, which contrasts with the usual straight-sided skyscrapers of the city.

Other museums display furniture, older art collections, personal art collections, history, and natural history. The Museum of the American Indian covers the history and

▲ Art collections like those of the Guggenheim (above) and the National Museum of the American Indian (below) attract large numbers of visitors.

culture of Native Americans and houses more than a million artifacts. New York residents and visitors have access to one of the largest ranges of cultural activity in the world. The city's many free concerts and plays allow people to enjoy cultural events, regardless of their incomes.

Getting outside

Participating in and watching sports is integral to many New Yorkers' lives. They have several good teams in a variety of sports, including baseball, basketball, hockey, and football. Although not everyone participates in a sport, many people watch the professionals. This can be by attending a game, watching on television at home, or viewing with others in one of the city's many sports bars, which have giant screens to show popular games.

Baseball games are often attended by families and are the best value for the money. Yankee Stadium in the Bronx is home to the New York Yankees, a top team. Their counterparts in Queens are the New York Mets, who play in Shea Stadium. The Knicks (short for Knickerbockers, a reference to the city's Dutch heritage) are an important basketball team. They play most of their games at Madison Square Garden, a large sports and entertainment

▲ Jogging in many of New York's parks is a popular way of keeping fit.

venue seating up to 20,000 people. This location is also home to the New York Rangers, the top ice hockey team.

For people who jog for exercise, the most popular location is around the Reservoir in Central Park. Bicyclists also ride there, as well as in Riverside Park, the East River Park, and Brooklyn's Prospect Park, and there are more than 60 miles of bike paths in the city. Croquet and chess can be played in Central Park. Cafés may also offer chess, although in Chinatown this might be replaced by games of mah-jongg. Apart from official sporting venues there are vacant lots where local youths play football or baseball or ride bikes. Skateboarding is a popular pastime, and the city's newly pedestrianized areas provide ideal locations for youths to practice their skills—an activity that is not always popular with the authorities or other local

◄ Young people often socialize through playing sports. Basketball is particularly popular.

At the beach

A day at the beach is easily reached from central New York by taking the subway out to Coney Island in Brooklyn. There are fairground rides and amusements alongside the wide beaches that face the Atlantic.

It can be crowded in the summer when people come in large numbers to escape the heat and stifling humidity of the city.

▼ Its wide beaches and pleasant sand make Coney Island beach a popular weekend destination.

The New York environment

Like all large cities, New York has to cope with an environment constantly strained by the overuse of resources and an ever-growing demand for the removal of waste products. New and creative responses to the demands of a growing population constantly need to be found to keep the city sustainable.

A thirsty city

When the City of New York was first settled the water supply came from shallow wells dug in Manhattan, but as the population increased there was a need to store water in order to have a continual supply. The first reservoir was built in 1776 when the city's population was about 22,000. By the middle of the 19th century authorities realized that much more water was needed, so the Croton River to the northwest was dammed. Aqueducts brought water into the city, and by the early 20th century water was also being brought in from the Catskill and Delaware watersheds, to the west of the city. Today there are 19 reservoirs and three

▼ New York draws much of its water from rivers and lakes to the northwest of the city.

controlled lakes providing water, plus some water pumped from aquifers (water-bearing rocks) in Queens and Brooklyn. Today 90 percent of the water comes from the Catskill/Delaware systems, with just under 10 percent from the Croton system. The water from the aquifer only provides about 1 percent of the water supply.

Water use in the city

The water supply system provides New Yorkers with 1.5 billion gallons of clean drinking water every day, 475 billion gallons a year. The Department of Environmental Protection (DEP) is responsible for the water supply and has to maintain the hundreds of miles of pipes and tunnels and the two largest underground storage tanks in the world. The DEP uses sonar (echo sounding) equipment to help detect leaks in the pipes; otherwise it would be difficult to trace leaks underneath roads and pavement. The DEP also encourages people to be less wasteful with their water use and limits some uses such as watering lawns. At present the city is constructing a huge new water tunnel, City Water Tunnel Number 3, to improve water delivery.

Wastewater

New York has 14 wastewater treatment plants, which require constant monitoring and maintenance. Wastewater comes from domestic and industrial uses, plus storm drainage. Sewage sludge is the solid waste left at the treatment plant after all the wastewater is processed. Until 1992 this was taken by barge and dumped in the ocean 12 miles offshore. Now much is taken out of the state and sprayed onto land as a fertilizer, composted, or placed in landfill sites.

In some areas, such as the south shore of Staten Island, a bluebelt system is used to treat some storm wastewater. Here, by allowing streams, ponds and wetlands to carry out their natural functions of carrying water, storing it, and filtering it through reeds, the city saves on costs and provides a natural landscape. Sixteen systems are already in place and others are planned. This is a more sustainable way of dealing with wastewater.

▼ One of the reservoirs from which New York City takes its water.

Garbage disposal

In 2005 the residents, schools, and hospitals of New York City produced nearly 68,000 tons of trash every week. This is more than 3.5 million tons a year, which is collected by the New York City Department of Sanitation (DOS). In addition, 2.2 million tons of waste for recycling was collected that year. On top of all this is the 13,000 tons of trash generated daily by commercial sources (4.7 million tons a year), but their waste is collected by private companies.

This is a gigantic amount of waste for any city to have to deal with, and it poses a serious problem if New York is to be sustainable. The DOS employs nearly 7,000 people and has a huge fleet of vehicles dedicated to keeping the city clean. While much of the waste produced in New York City is recycled, the proportion is low compared with other cities of a similar size, such as Los Angeles, which recycles about 40 percent. Until 2001 garbage was taken by barge to Fresh Kills on Staten Island (see page 53) to be put into a huge landfill site. Now that site is closed, and the trash is taken to landfill sites in other states, some as far as 300 miles away. Although some of the trash could be incinerated (burned) it would produce too many harmful gases and toxins. New Yorkers are being encouraged to "Reduce, Reuse, and Recycle," but there is much work to be done in reducing waste.

▼ If trash is not collected quickly it attracts rats and other vermin, causing a possible health hazard.

The Fresh Kills landfill

The landfill site at Fresh Kills opened in 1948 on a 2,200-acre area of open land and wetlands. It took in thousands of tons of garbage a day, forming four huge mounds, one as tall as the Statue of Liberty. The landfill site is so large it can be seen from space! The site was unlined, so over time thousands of gallons of toxic wastes have leached into the local watercourses. Eventually the city realized that the landfill was badly damaging the environment of Staten Island and the site was closed. It had to reopen briefly to take the debris from the destruction of the World Trade Center. This debris was carefully sorted on site to check for human remains. Part of the plans for the area include a memorial to those who died. Now that Fresh Kills is fully closed as a landfill site, plans are under way to turn it into a large-scale park. The wetland areas are to be preserved and the waste mounds are to be landscaped to create an attractive recreational area with access to rivers and the ocean.

▼ Posters encourage New Yorkers to recycle most types of waste in order to reduce disposal costs.

▼ Huge amounts of cardboard used in stores in the city are now recycled.

Caring for the environment

New Yorkers are becoming more aware of their impact on the environment. Many realize that individuals need to make changes to their lifestyles in order to limit their impact on the city's environment. There are several groups working to help build community gardens on neglected sites, and others that organize the recycling of kitchen and garden waste. The New York Restoration Project was started in 1995 by the actress Bette Midler, with the goal of developing small vacant lots into communal gardens. Such gardens can help a neighborhood to work together, and in many cases petty vandalism is reduced. When local people are involved in creating a garden it tends to be well looked after because they feel a sense of ownership.

▲ The Adopt-a-Highway program encourages local organizations to undertake regular litter removal along a certain stretch of road, in return for the publicity, when the group's name is put up by the road.

▼ Community gardens improve the local environment for everyone, providing green spaces in many crowded areas of the city.

In a large city like New York it is not always easy to recycle organic material, such as kitchen or garden wastes. On the Lower East Side of Manhattan individual residents are able to send their compostable waste to the Compost Education Center. The center accepts organic waste from local residents, then turns it into compost which can then be sold to local gardeners to cover costs. In the future similar methods will become more necessary as the city works to reduce the amount of waste it has to remove.

Jamaica Bay

A 9,100-acre area of wetlands, Jamaica Bay lies on the southern shores of Brooklyn and Queens, near JFK Airport. Until the late 20th century it was used as a landfill, and parts were drained and used for commercial development. It was largely ignored as an area of open recreational space. Three quarters of the wetlands area are now gone, but what is left is important for migrating birds and as a general wetland habitat. The area is now known as the Jamaica Bay Wildlife Refuge and is part of the Gateway National Recreation Area. An open and wild landscape, it is only a subway ride away from Manhattan and many New Yorkers take advantage of the location to get closer to nature.

▼ The Jamaica Bay wetlands, off Brooklyn and Queens.

CASE STUDY

Sally Young, garden organizer

Sally helps organize the community garden at 6th Street and Avenue B. Community gardens help people to come together to work for a common cause. "There are hundreds of community gardens all over New York using unused or derelict land. Some are pretty organized, like ours, with members and committees; others are simple little plots on waste ground. But we're all doing our bit for biodiversity in a city most known for its streets, traffic horrors, and nightlife. We have all worked so hard to make this the place you see today—a tiny haven for people and wildlife, especially butterflies, amid the noise and bustle of a huge city. Each member has a little plot and can grow whatever they like: flowers, vegetables, or even nurturing the wild plants that spring up on their own."

The New York of tomorrow

New York is a large city and it is difficult for it to be truly sustainable. New York has to import large amounts of water, food, and energy into its boundaries, and the area it needs to draw on in order to have these essentials is vast. But the city is working to reduce its resource demands.

In the future there will need to be larger numbers of the fuel-efficient buses and subways, but more will have to be done to reduce car use in the city center. New zoning measures help to protect public health by separating industrial and residential uses. There are more residential developments in the city center, encouraging young professionals back into areas abandoned in previous decades. Living near one's place of work is a more sustainable option and means less car use. As fossil fuels run out people may not have the choice of being able to commute long distances to work. New York plans to attract new industries in the future by helping to fund science parks today, where new ideas may lead to more high-tech jobs for the city.

Recycling of wastes continues to be encouraged, but some feel that in the future there should be a tax on all throwaway products such as plastic cups. This would help fund waste disposal, although it would be far better to make everything recyclable or reusable. Green space will continue to have importance in all planned developments but also at a local level where people work together to

▼ Onlookers reading about the events at Ground Zero, the site of the destruction of the World Trade Center. A new tower will be built on the site.

▲ A film crew documents an event highlighting the use of cleaner fuels in New York taxis, helping to improve the air quality of the city.

produce community gardens. The future will see the completion of the greening of the city's waterfront edges and the opening of the High Line (see page 41) as a green walkway.

Reduced car use, less waste, more greenery, and better air quality are achievable goals for the city, but they will not be easy. They will require changes not only in the way the city is run, but also in the way that the people of the city view the importance of good citizenship.

▶ Kids on the block. "New York is a great place to live and we can't think of spending our lives anyplace else."

Glossary

aquifer A layer of porous rock that holds water.

biodiversity The variety of species found within an area.

birthrate The number of births per thousand population.

brownfield A site that has already been used in the past, polluted, and then abandoned.

brownstone houses Houses built in the 19th century from the local New York sandstone, which is brown.

death rate The number of deaths per thousand population.

emigrant A person who leaves his or her country of birth to live and work in another country.

gentrification The process by which an urban area that was home to low-income groups is settled by people with higher incomes. They then upgrade the houses and the area changes character.

ghetto A clearly defined city district where there is a concentration of a particular group of people linked by common religion, race, or country of origin.

Great Depression A period that began in 1929 when the New York stock market crashed. There were huge job losses around the country and people lost a lot of money. It lasted until the beginning of World War II.

high-tech industries Industries that use the latest production techniques and technology.

immigrant A person who settles in a new country.

migrant A general term for a person who moves to a new area for work or education.

multicultural Characterized by the presence of many racial groups, nationalities, and cultures.

pedestrianization The process of closing a street or an area to motor vehicles, making it easier for people on foot.

primary industry Any extractive industry, such as mining, agriculture, forestry, fishing, and quarrying.

retailing The service industry involved in the selling goods to the public.

regeneration The process of improving a rundown urban area. Decision makers such as city councils invest in the area to create a better living and working environment to attract businesses and residents and help drive its recovery forward.

reservoir An artificial lake created to store water.

secondary industry Industries that use raw materials to manufacture goods.

service industry Industries that provide services for people and companies, such as taxis, banks, and stores.

suburbs The outer areas of a city, where housing dominates.

suburbanization The process by which people move out from the city center to live in the outer areas; they often return to the center for work and entertainment.

subway The system of electric, mostly underground trains of New York City.

tenement An early form of apartment building used in the 19th century to house those on low incomes. Few remain because they were poorly planned, crowded, and poorly ventilated.

urbanization The movement of people from rural to urban areas.

urban sprawl The unplanned outward growth of towns and cities.

watershed The land from which a watercourse gets its water as precipitation falls on it and drains downhill.

Further information

Useful Web sites

New York City Department of City Planning
http://www.nyc.gov/html/dcp/
New plans for the future of all five boroughs.

NYC & Company
http://www.nycvisit.com/home/index.cfm
The city's official tourism Web site, with much up-to-date information about what is happening in New York City.

NYC.gov
http://www.nyc.gov/portal/index.jsp?front_door=true
The official Web site of New York City, with many links to city departments and a useful Frequently Asked Questions page.

The Tenement Encyclopedia
http://www.tenement.org/encyclopedia/
A fact-filled online book that describes the housing and day-to-day life in a historic immigrant neighborhood.

Books

Labi, Esther. *New York*. Eyewitness Travel Guides. New York: Dorling Kindersley, 2003.
An information-packed guide to the Big Apple, filled with color photographs.

New York Transit Museum. *Subway Style*. New York: Stewart, Tabori & Chang, 2004.
A lavishly illustrated history of the origin and development of New York City's subway stations and trains.

Ogintz, Eileen. *The Kid's Guide to New York City*. Guilford, Conn.: Globe Pequot, 2004.
A guide to the city's foods, cultures, shopping, and entertainment, for readers age 9 to 12.

Taylor, Sydney. *All-of-a-Kind Family*. New York: Delacorte, 2005.
A novel set in early 20th-century New York about the daughters in a Jewish family. Although written for a younger audience, all ages can enjoy this story, with its many references to New York locations.

Index

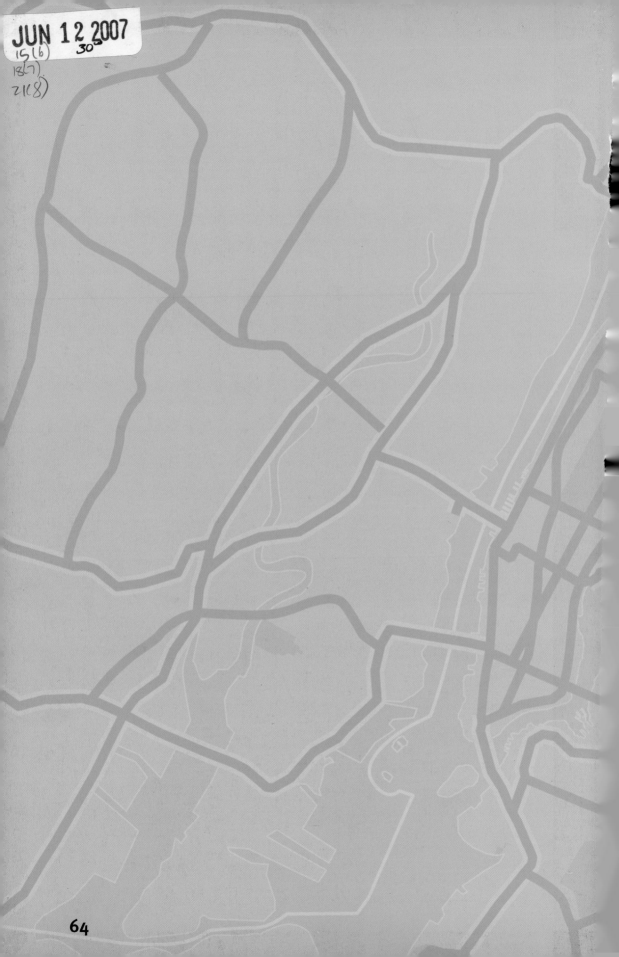